THIS 2025 DESK CALENDAR BELONGS TO:

____

____

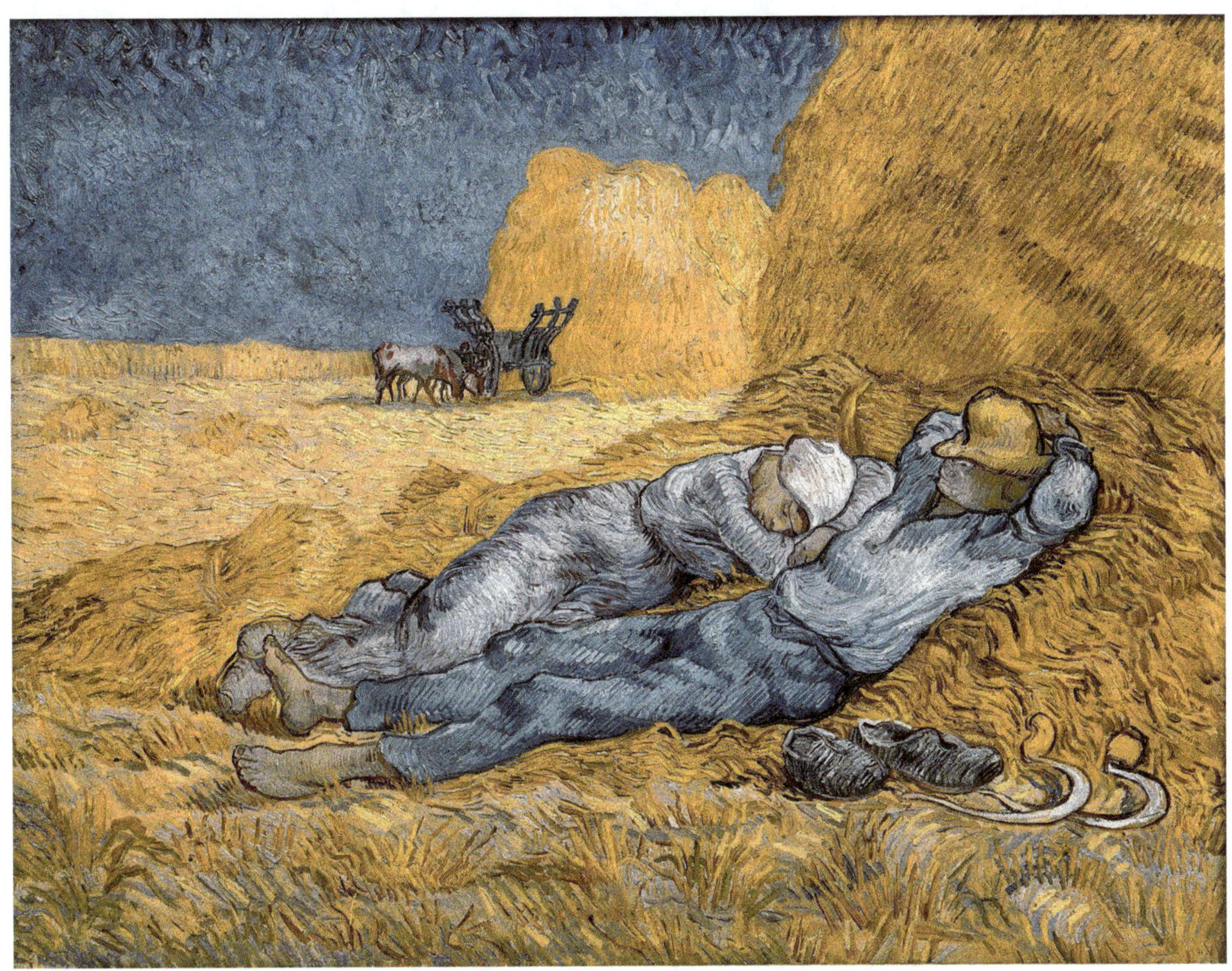

Noon Rest At Work, 1890 by Vincent Van Gogh

January | 2025

GOALS

SUNDAY	MONDAY	TUESDAY	WEDNESDAY	THURSDAY	FRIDAY	SATURDAY
			1 New Year's Day	2	3	4
5	6	7	8	9	10	11
12	13	14	15	16	17	18
19	20 Martin Luther King Jr. Day	21	22	23	24	25
26	27	28	29 Chinese New Year	30	31	

NOTES

TO DO LIST

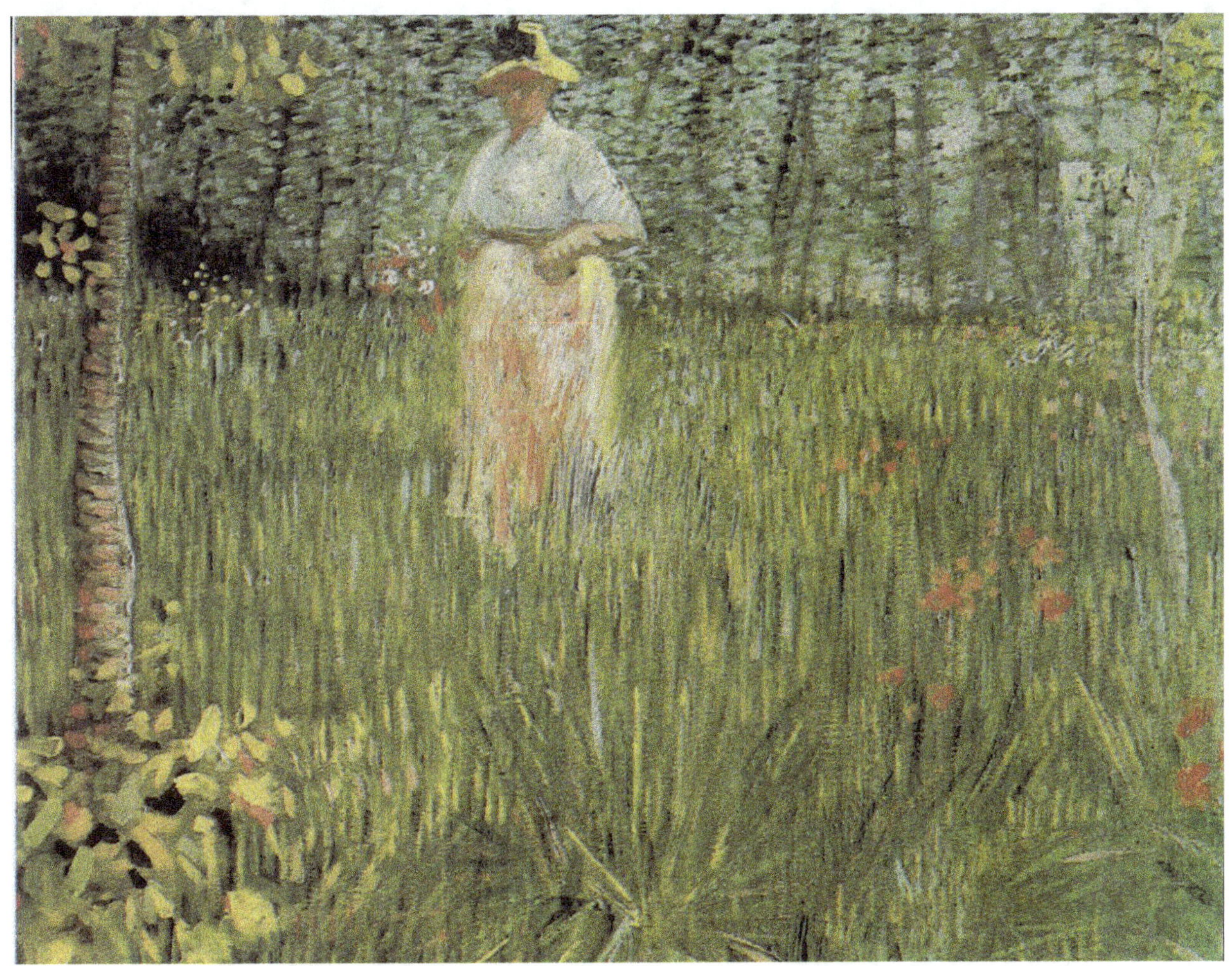

A Woman Walking In a Garden, 1887 by Vincent Van Gogh

FEBRUARY | 2025

GOALS

NOTES

TO DO LIST

SUNDAY	MONDAY	TUESDAY	WEDNESDAY	THURSDAY	FRIDAY	SATURDAY
						1
2	3	4	5	6	7	8
9	10	11	12	13	14 Valentine's Day	15
16	17 President's Day	18	19	20	21	22
23	24	25	26	27	28	

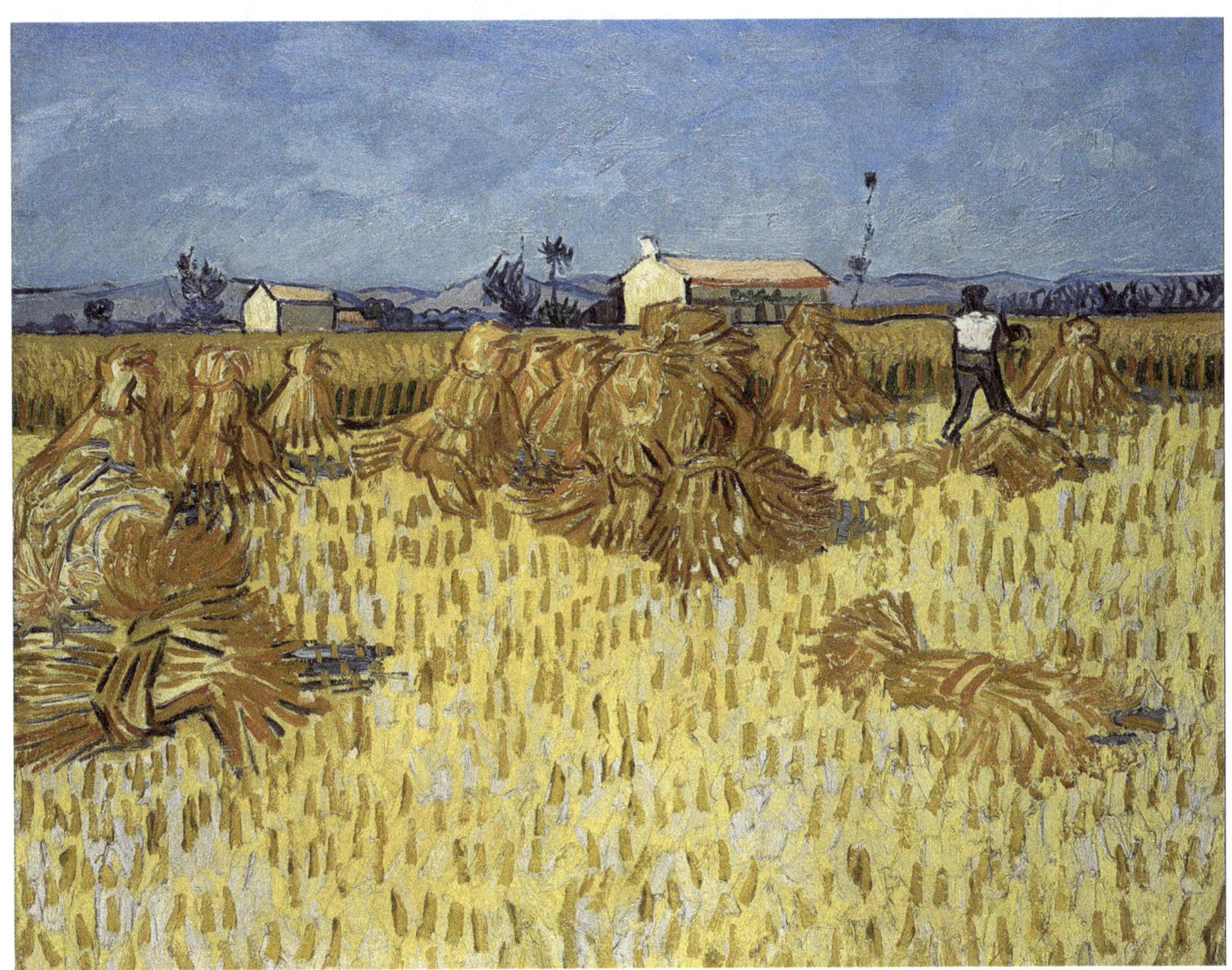

The Sower, 1888 by Vincent Van Gogh

March | 2025

SUNDAY	MONDAY	TUESDAY	WEDNESDAY	THURSDAY	FRIDAY	SATURDAY
						1
2	3	4	5 Ash Wednesday	6	7	8
9	10	11	12	13	14	15
16	17 St. Patrick's Day	18	19	20	21	22
23	24	25	26	27	28	29
30	31					

GOALS

NOTES

TO DO LIST

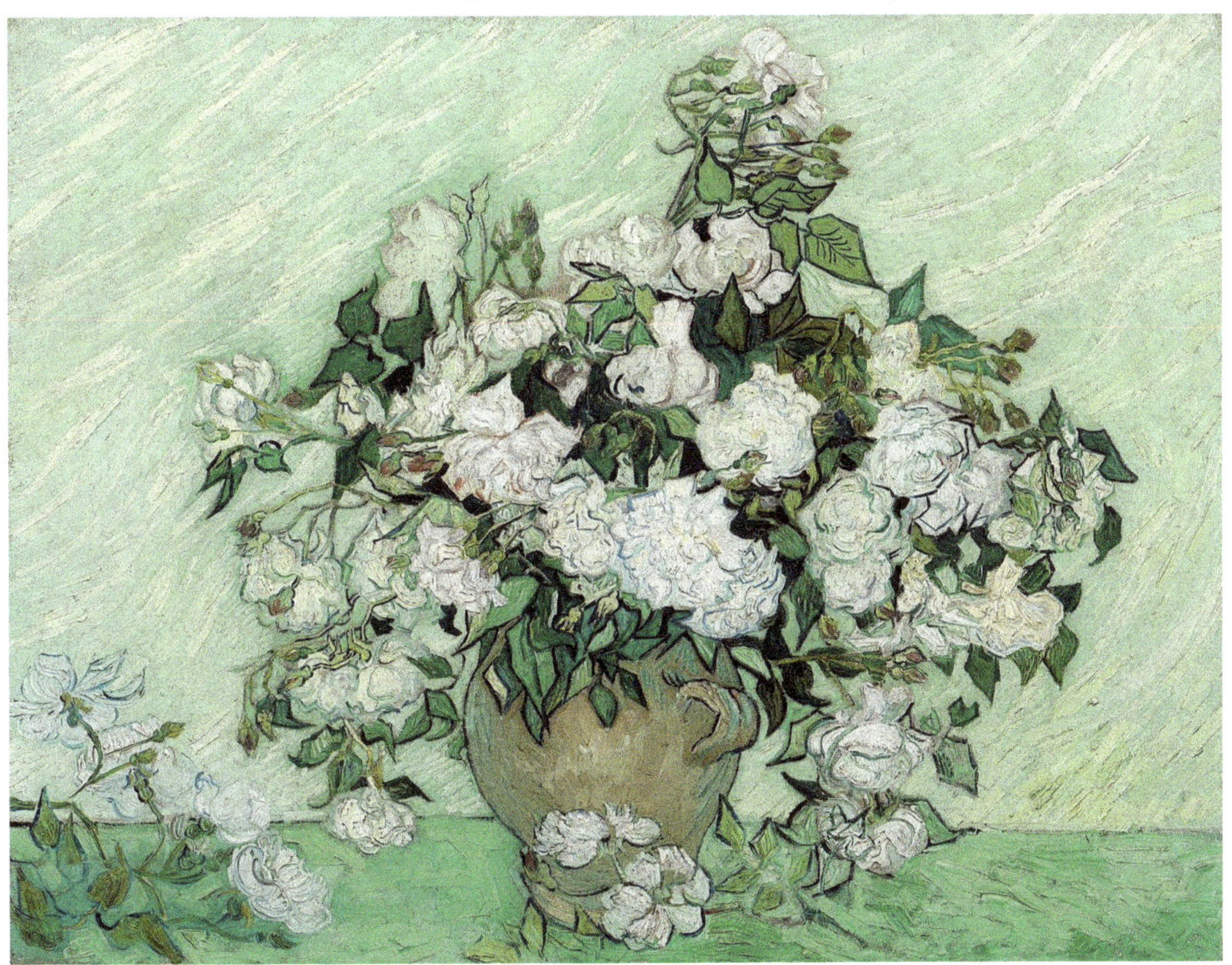

Roses, 1890 by Vincent Van Gogh

April | 2025

SUNDAY	MONDAY	TUESDAY	WEDNESDAY	THURSDAY	FRIDAY	SATURDAY
		1 April Fool's Day	2	3	4	5
6	7	8	9	10	11	12
13 Passover	14	15	16	17	18	19
20 Easter	21	22 Earth Day	23	24	25	26
27	28	29	30			

GOALS

NOTES

TO DO LIST

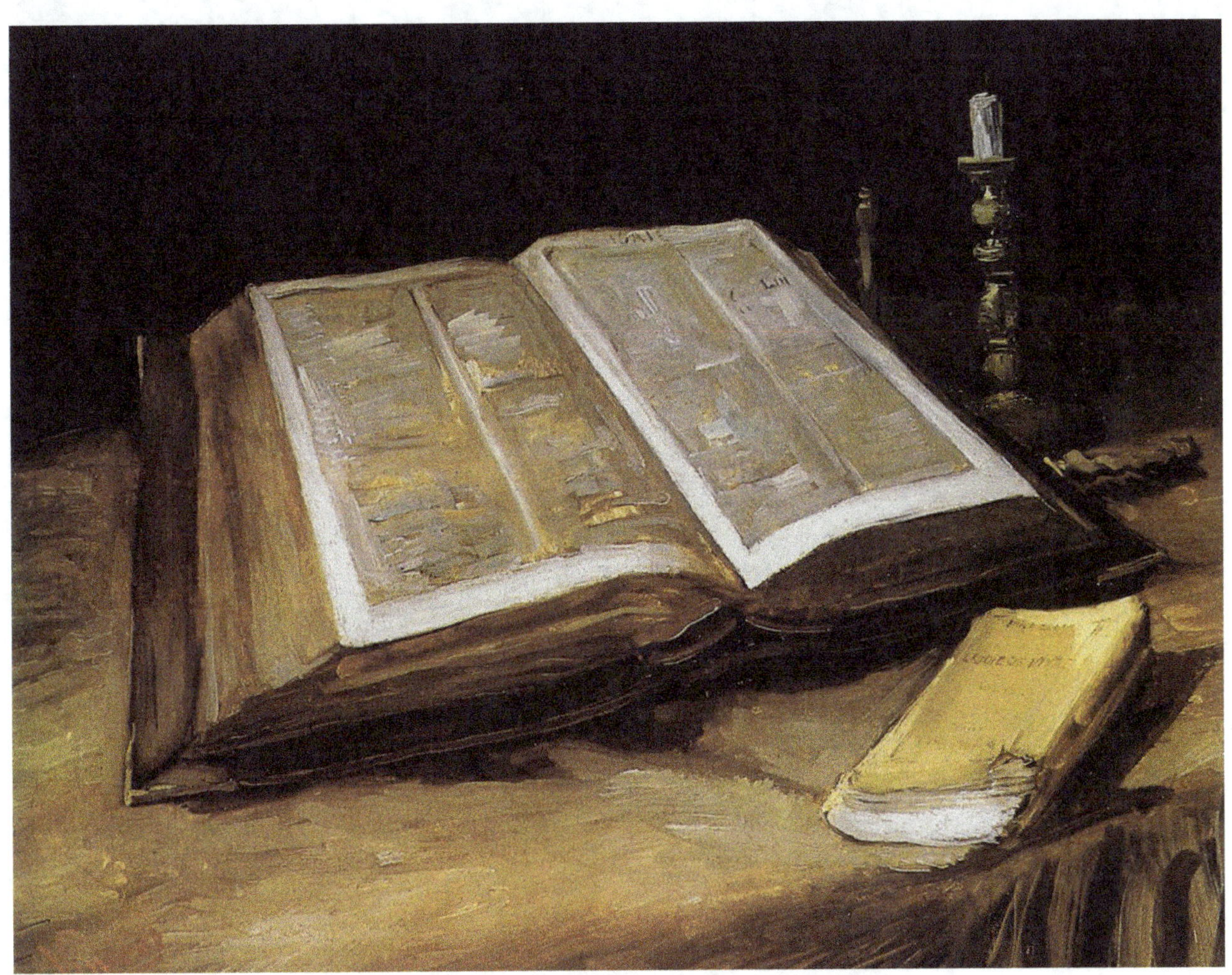

STILL LIFE WITH BIBLE, 1885 BY VINCENT VAN GOGH

MAY | 2025

GOALS	SUNDAY	MONDAY	TUESDAY	WEDNESDAY	THURSDAY	FRIDAY	SATURDAY
					1	2	3
	4	5 Cinco de Mayo	6	7	8	9	10
NOTES	11 Mother's Day	12	13	14	15	16	17
	18	19	20	21	22	23	24
TO DO LIST	25	26 Memorial Day	27	28	29	30	31

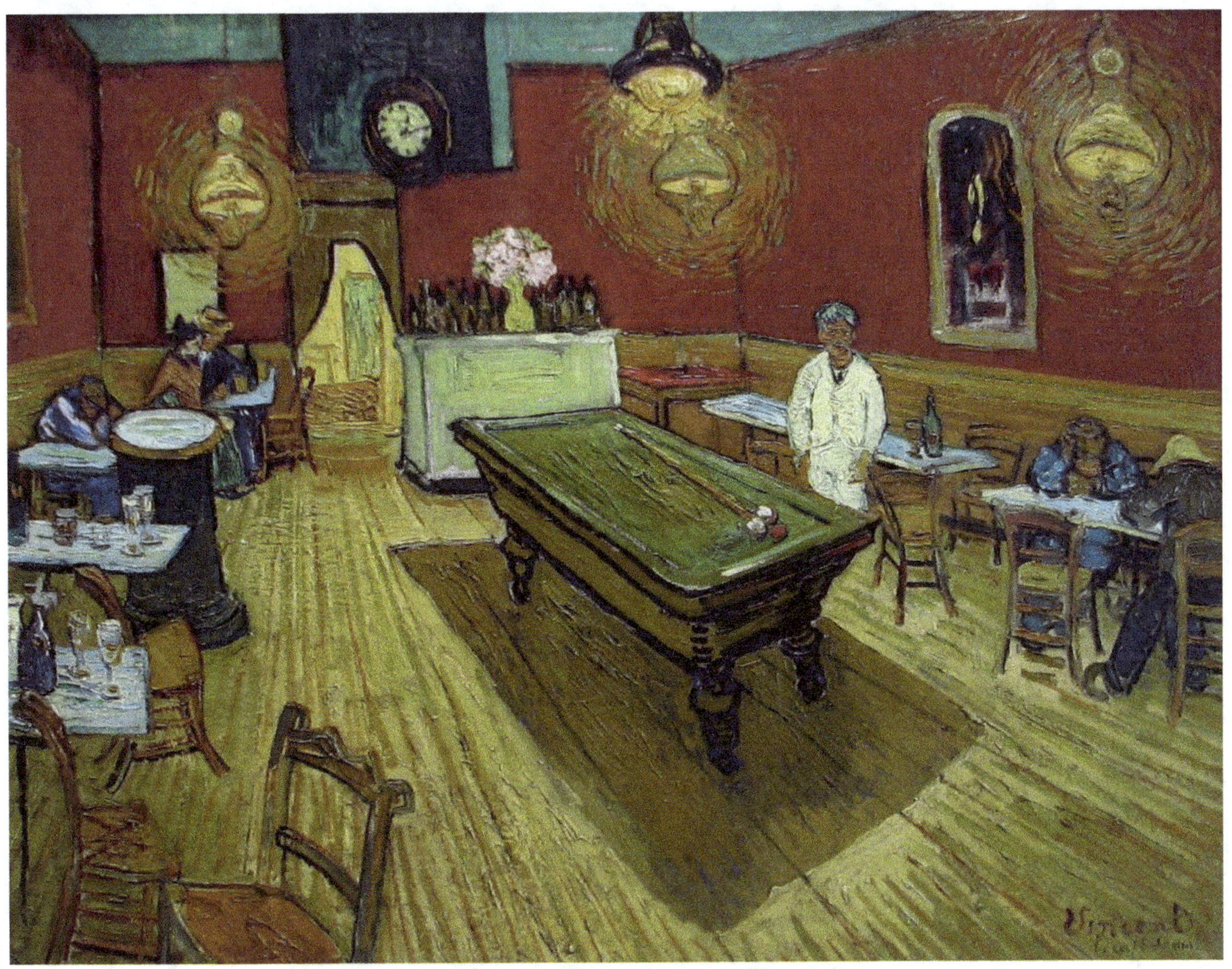
The Night Cafe, 1888 by Vincent Van Gogh

JUNE | 2025

SUNDAY	MONDAY	TUESDAY	WEDNESDAY	THURSDAY	FRIDAY	SATURDAY
1	2	3	4	5	6	7
8 Pentecost	9	10	11	12	13	14 Flag Day
15 Father's Day	16	17	18	19 Juneteenth	20	21 June Solstice
22	23	24	25	26	27	28
29	30					

GOALS

NOTES

TO DO LIST

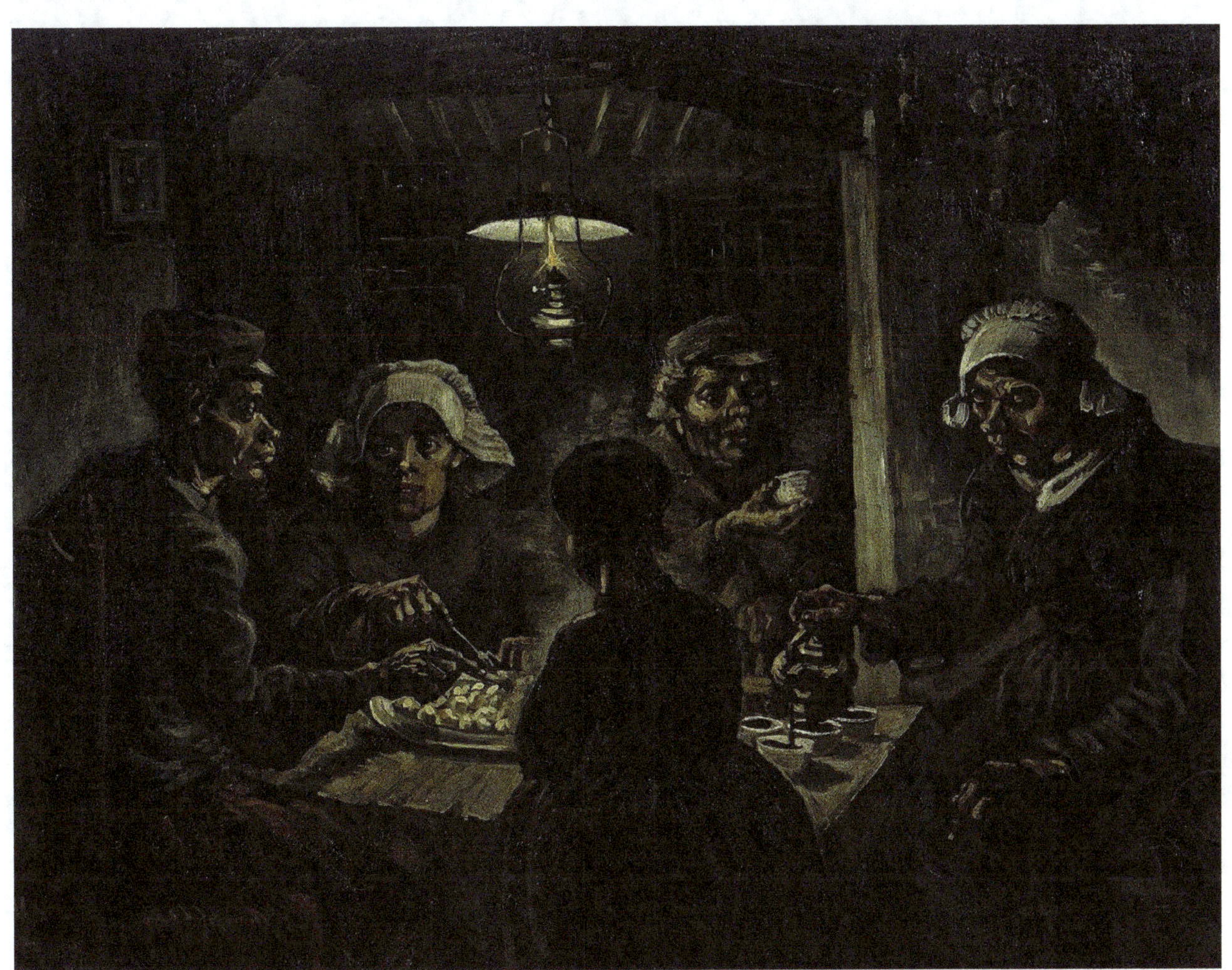

The Potato Eaters, 1885 by Vincent Van Gogh

July | 2025

GOALS

NOTES

TO DO LIST

SUNDAY	MONDAY	TUESDAY	WEDNESDAY	THURSDAY	FRIDAY	SATURDAY
		1	2	3	4 Independence Day	5
6	7	8	9	10	11	12
13	14	15	16	17	18	19
20	21	22	23	24	25	26
27	28	29	30	31		

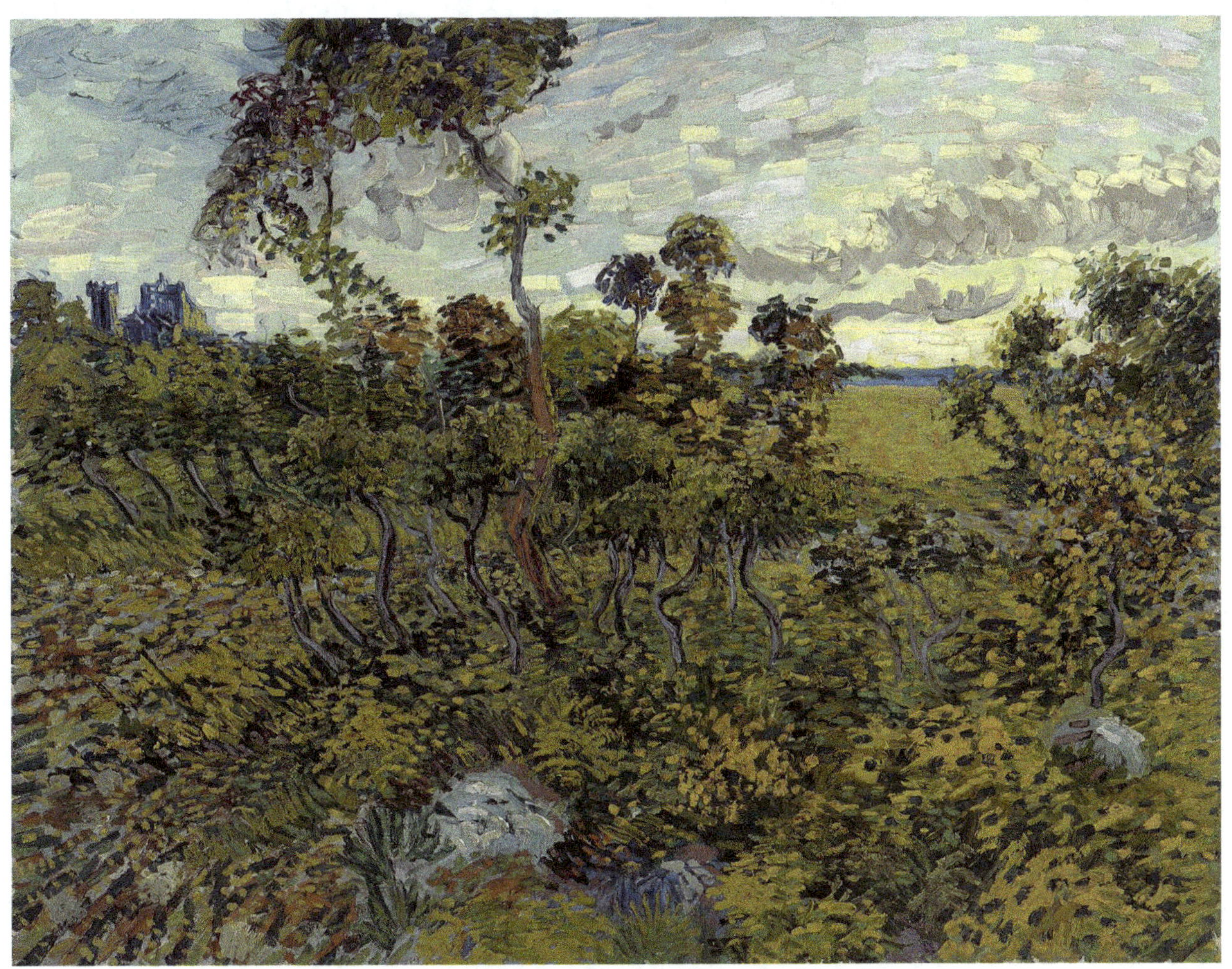

Sunset at Montmajour, 1888 by Vincent Van Gogh

August | 2025

GOALS

NOTES

TO DO LIST

SUNDAY	MONDAY	TUESDAY	WEDNESDAY	THURSDAY	FRIDAY	SATURDAY
					1	2
3	4	5	6	7	8	9
10	11	12	13	14	15	16
17	18	19	20	21	22	23
24	25	26	27	28	29	30
31						

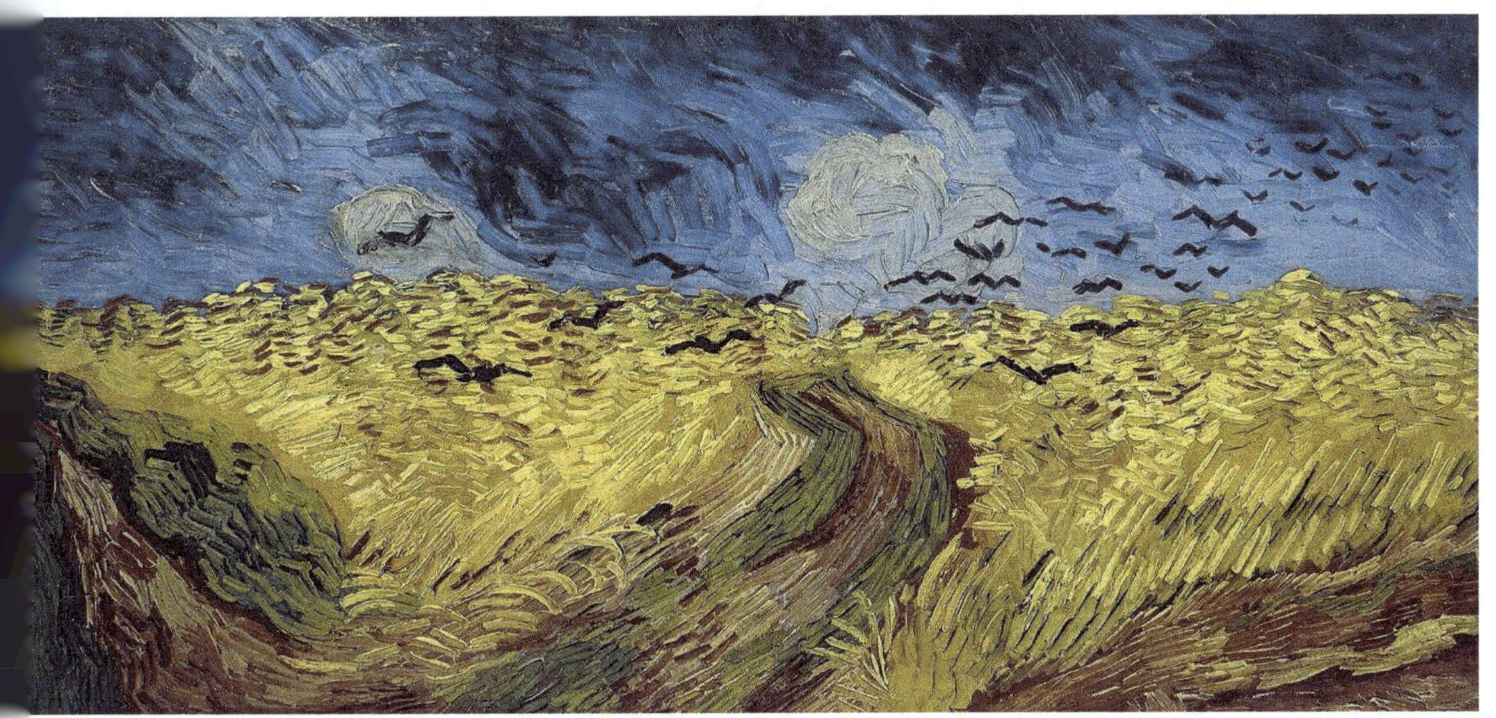

WHEATFIELD WITH CROWS, 1890 BY VINCENT VAN GOGH

SEPTEMBER | 2025

SUNDAY	MONDAY	TUESDAY	WEDNESDAY	THURSDAY	FRIDAY	SATURDAY
	1 Labor Day	2	3	4	5	6
7 Grandparents Day	8	9	10	11	12	13
14	15	16	17	18	19	20
21	22	23 Rosh Hashanah	24	25	26	27
28	29	30				

GOALS

NOTES

TO DO LIST

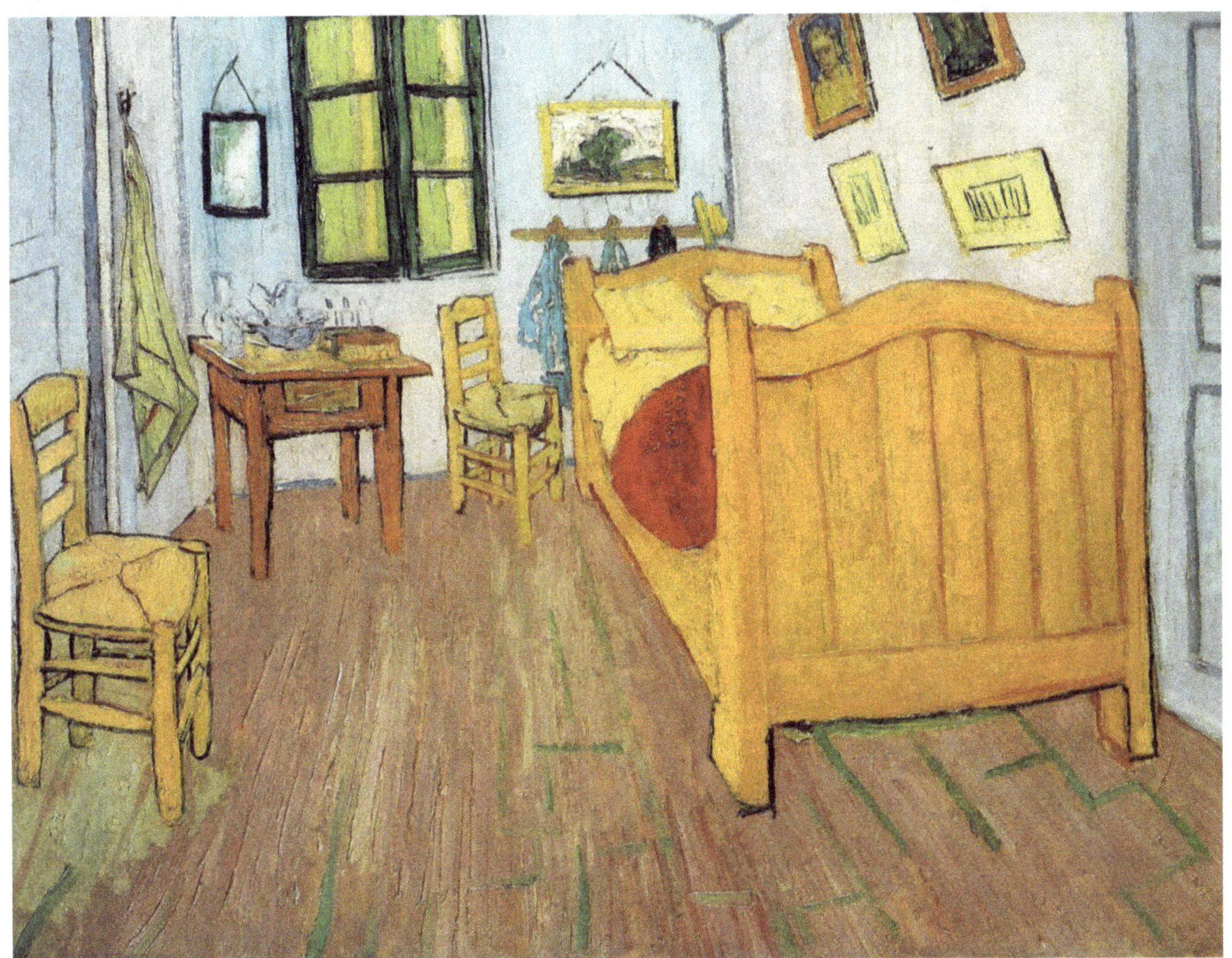

The Bedroom, 1888 by Vincent Van Gogh

October | 2025

GOALS

NOTES

TO DO LIST

SUNDAY	MONDAY	TUESDAY	WEDNESDAY	THURSDAY	FRIDAY	SATURDAY
			1	2	3	4
5	6	7	8	9	10	11
12	13	14	15	16	17	18
19	20	21	22	23	24	25
26	27	28	29	30	31 Halloween	

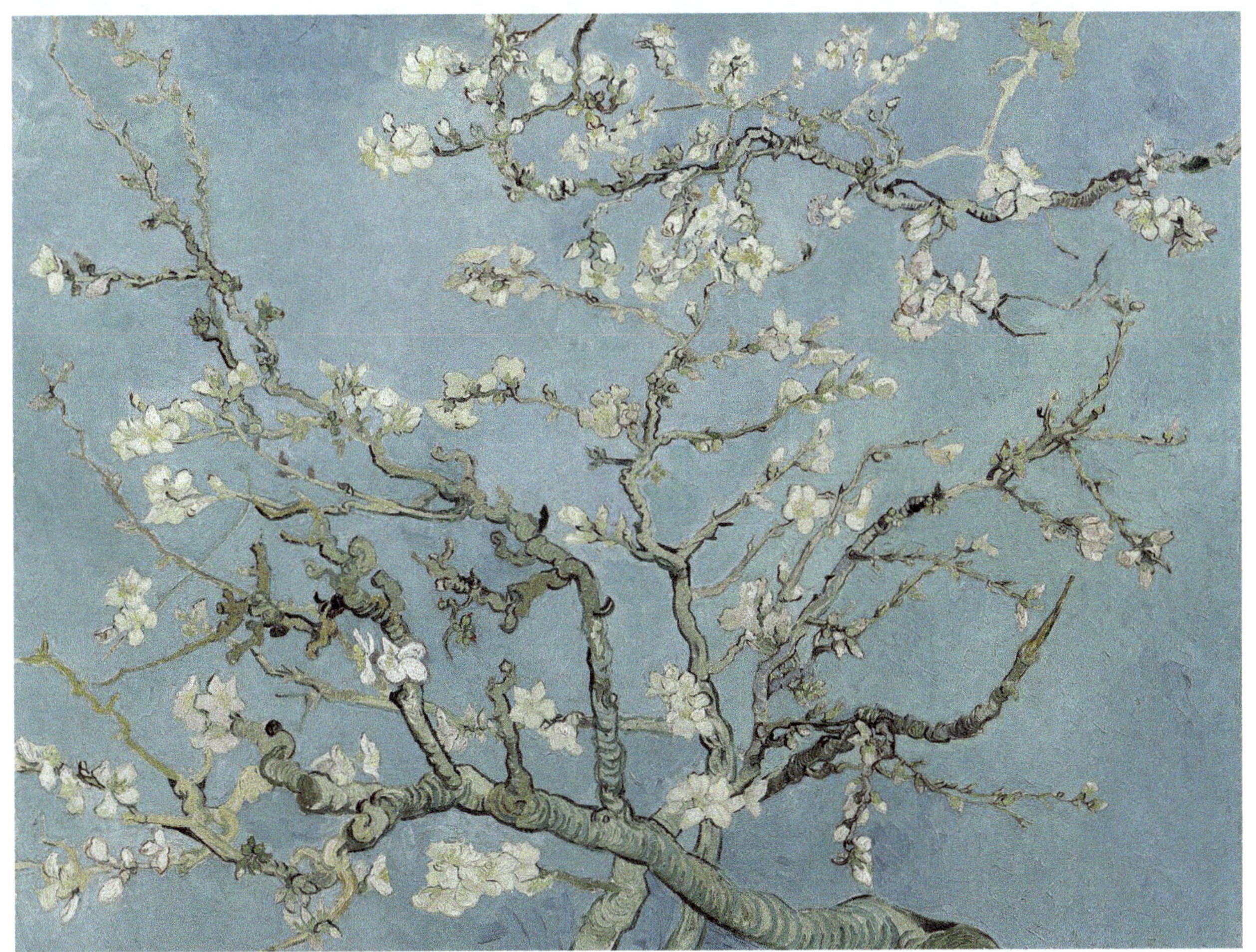

Almond Blossoms, 1890 by Vincent Van Gogh

November | 2025

SUNDAY	MONDAY	TUESDAY	WEDNESDAY	THURSDAY	FRIDAY	SATURDAY
			1	2	3	4
5	6	7	8	9	10	11 Veterans Day
12	13	14	15	16	17	18
19	20	21	22	23	24	25
26	27 Thanksgiving	28	29	30	31	

GOALS

NOTES

TO DO LIST

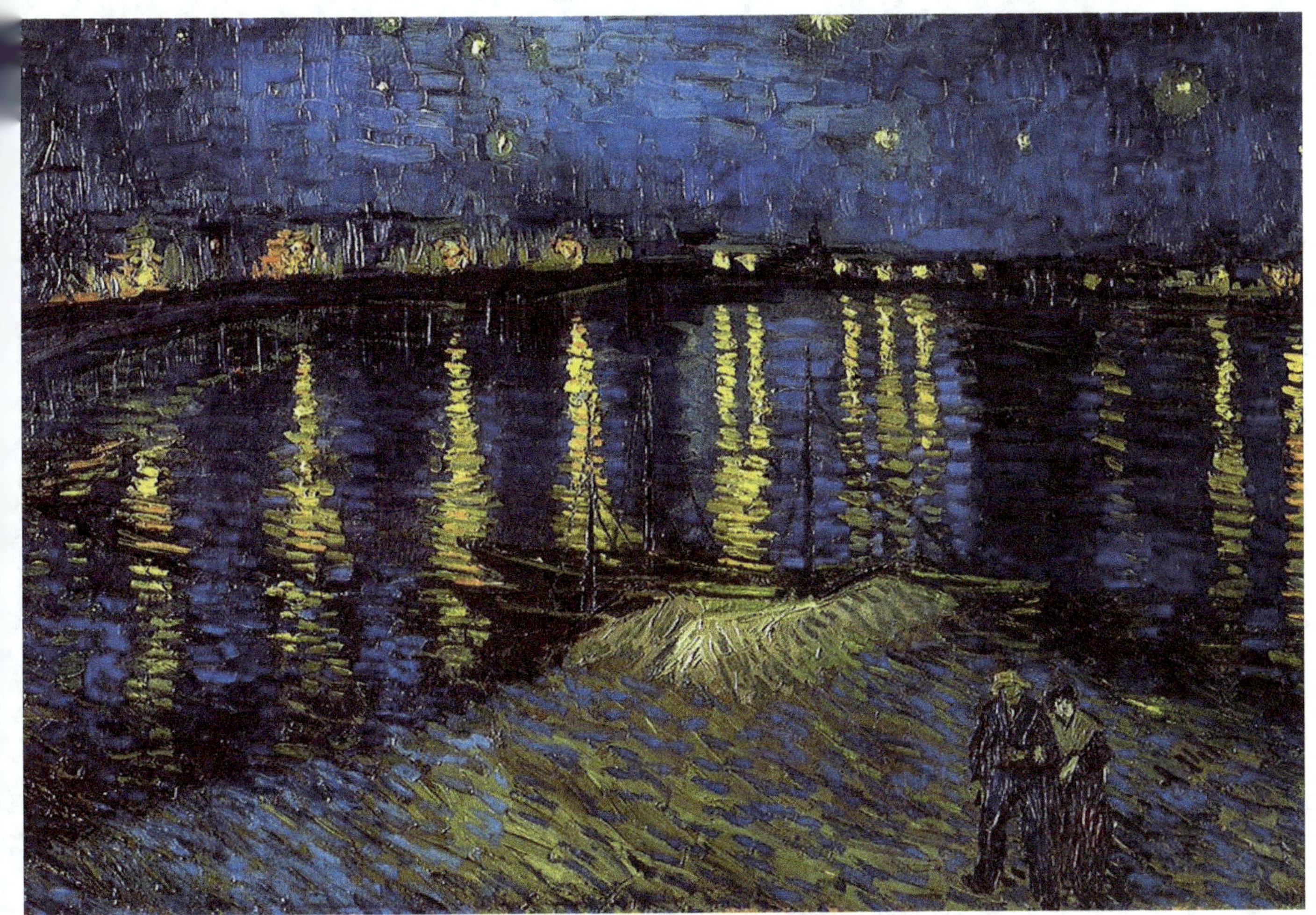

Starry Night Over The Rhone, 1888 by Vincent Van Gogh

December | 2025

SUNDAY	MONDAY	TUESDAY	WEDNESDAY	THURSDAY	FRIDAY	SATURDAY
	1	2	3	4	5	6
7	8	9	10	11	12	13
14 Hanukkah begins	15	16	17	18	19	20
21 December Solstice	22	23	24 Christmas Eve	25 Christmas Day	26 Kwanzaa begins	27
28	29	30	31 New Year's Eve			

GOALS

NOTES

TO DO LIST